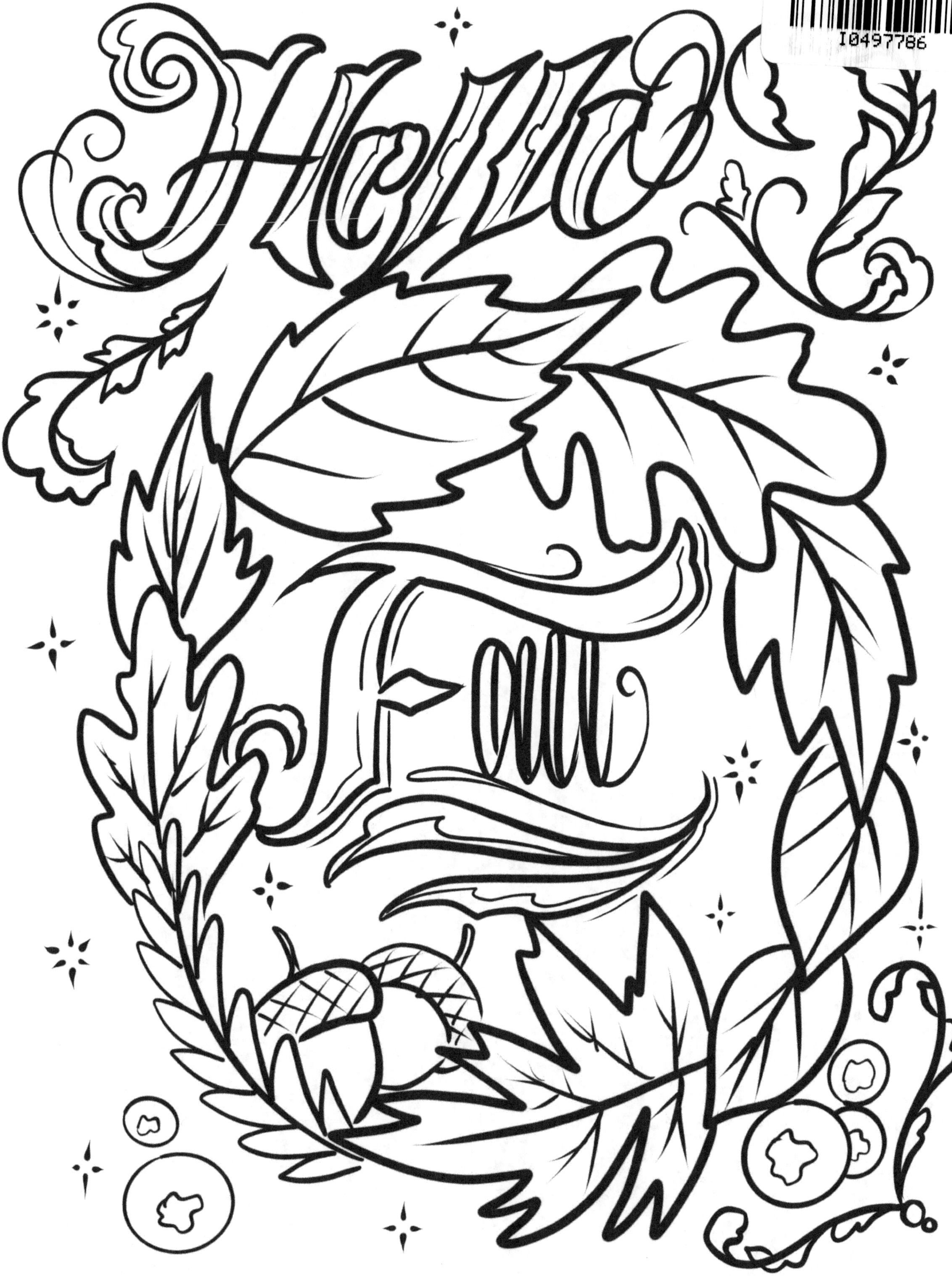
Hello
Fall

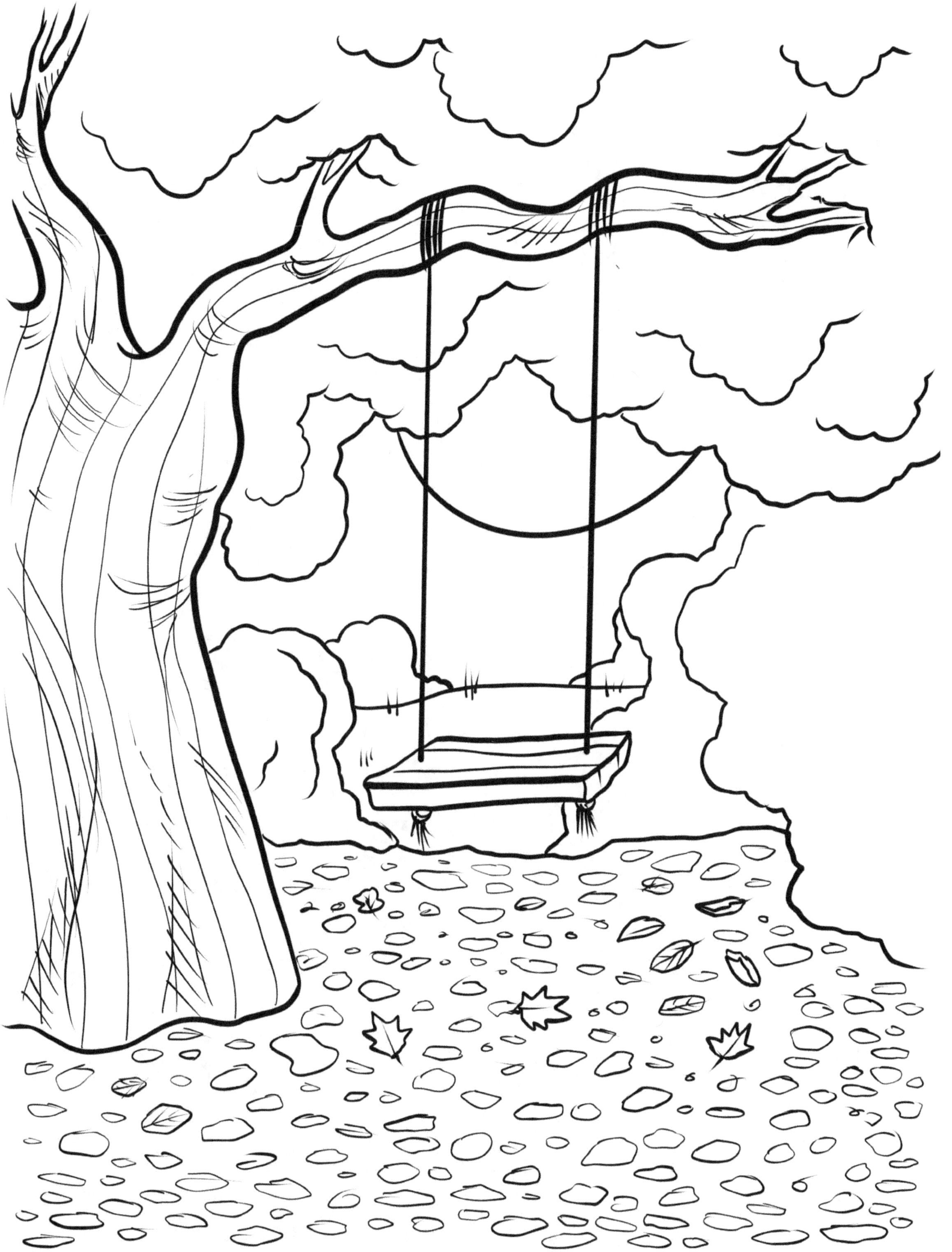

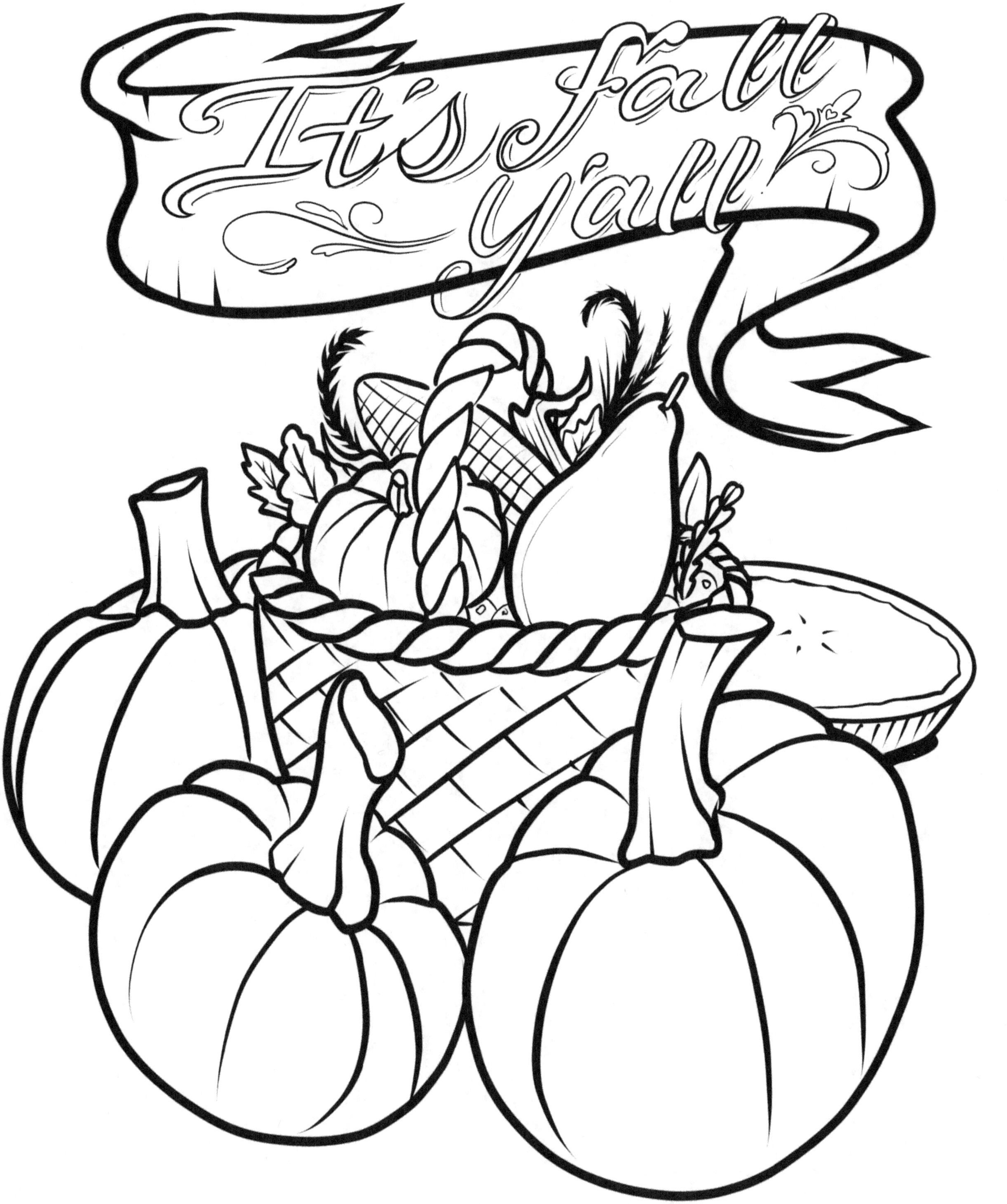
It's fall y'all

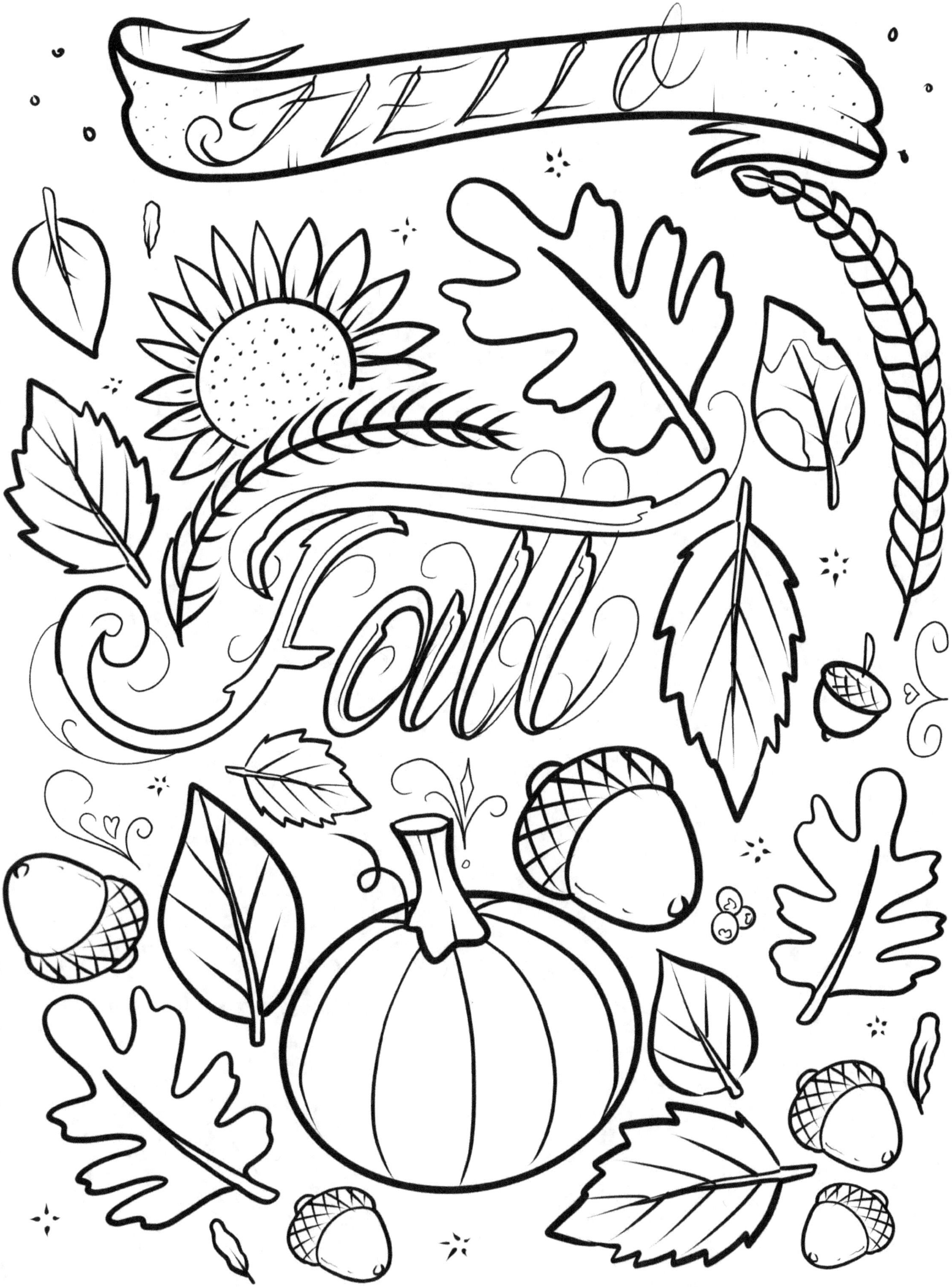
Hello
Fall

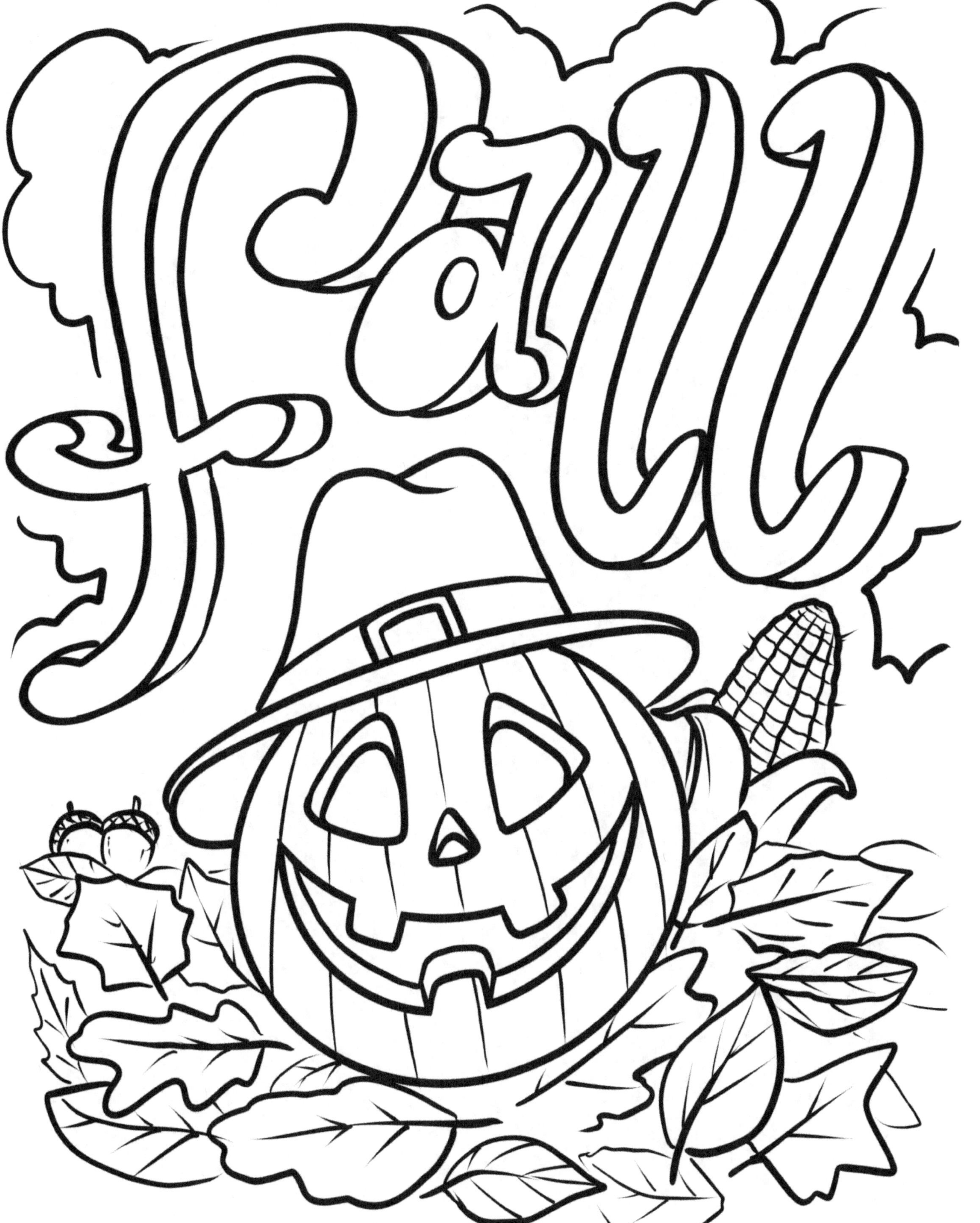
Fall

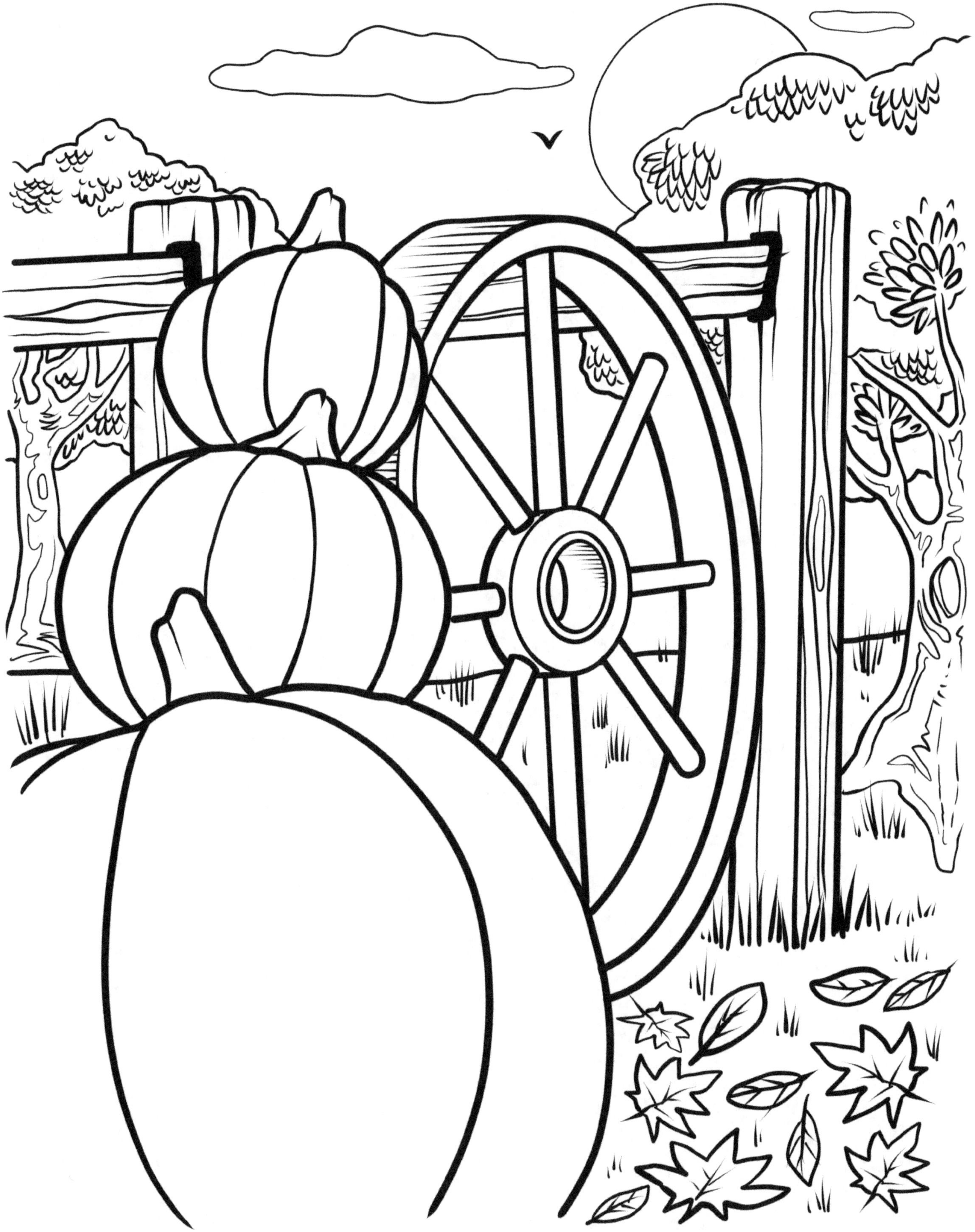

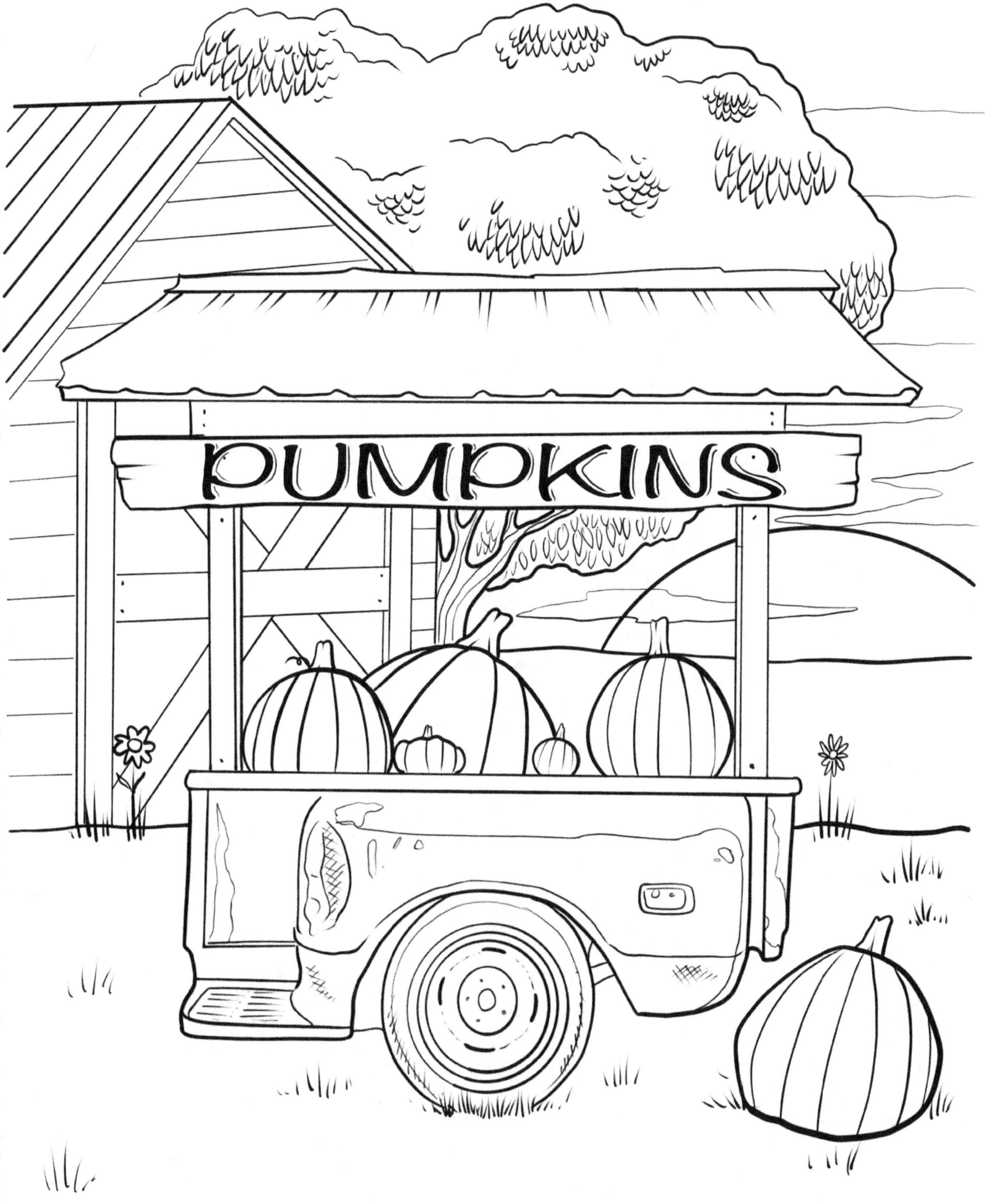
PUMPKINS

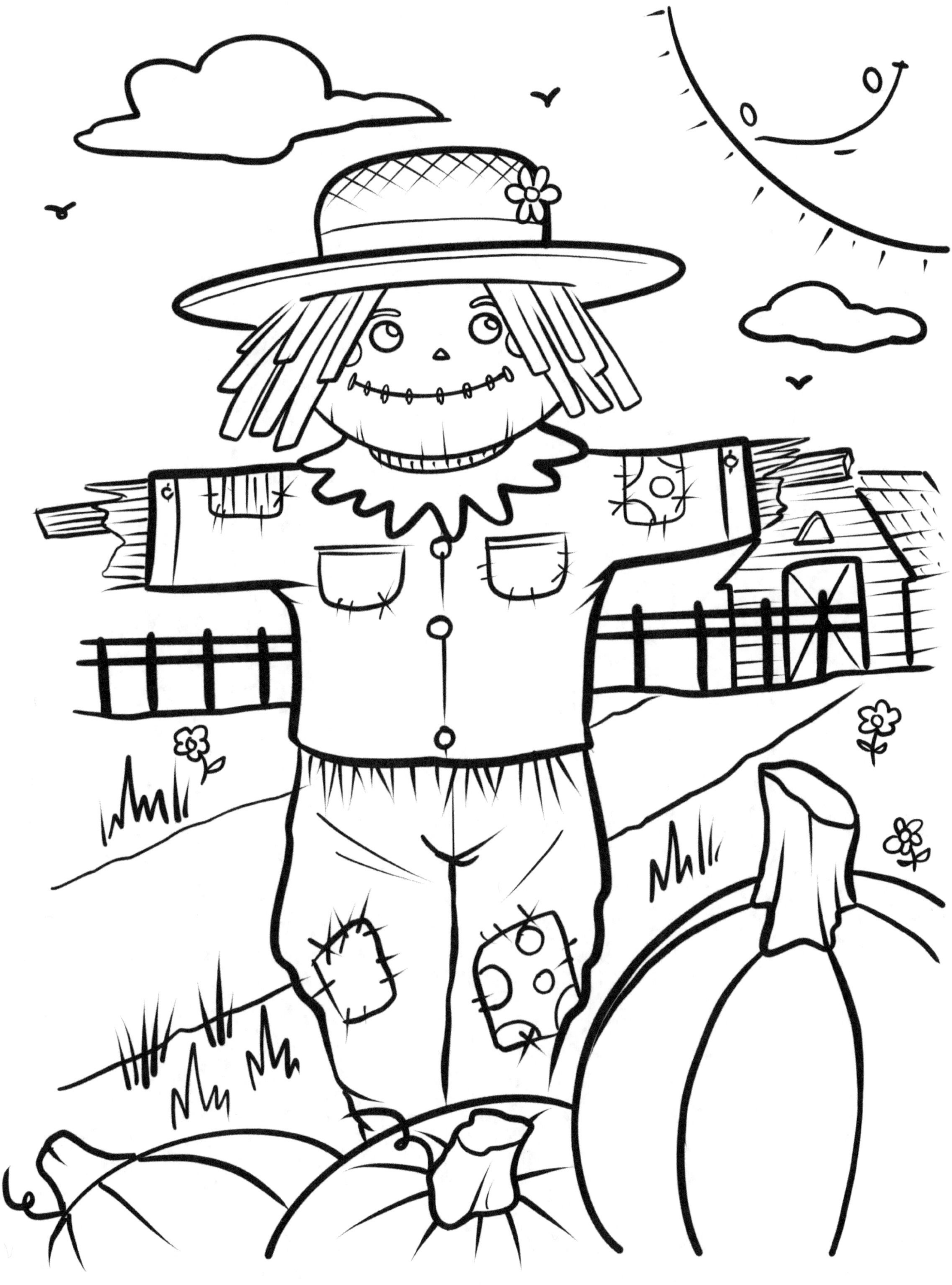

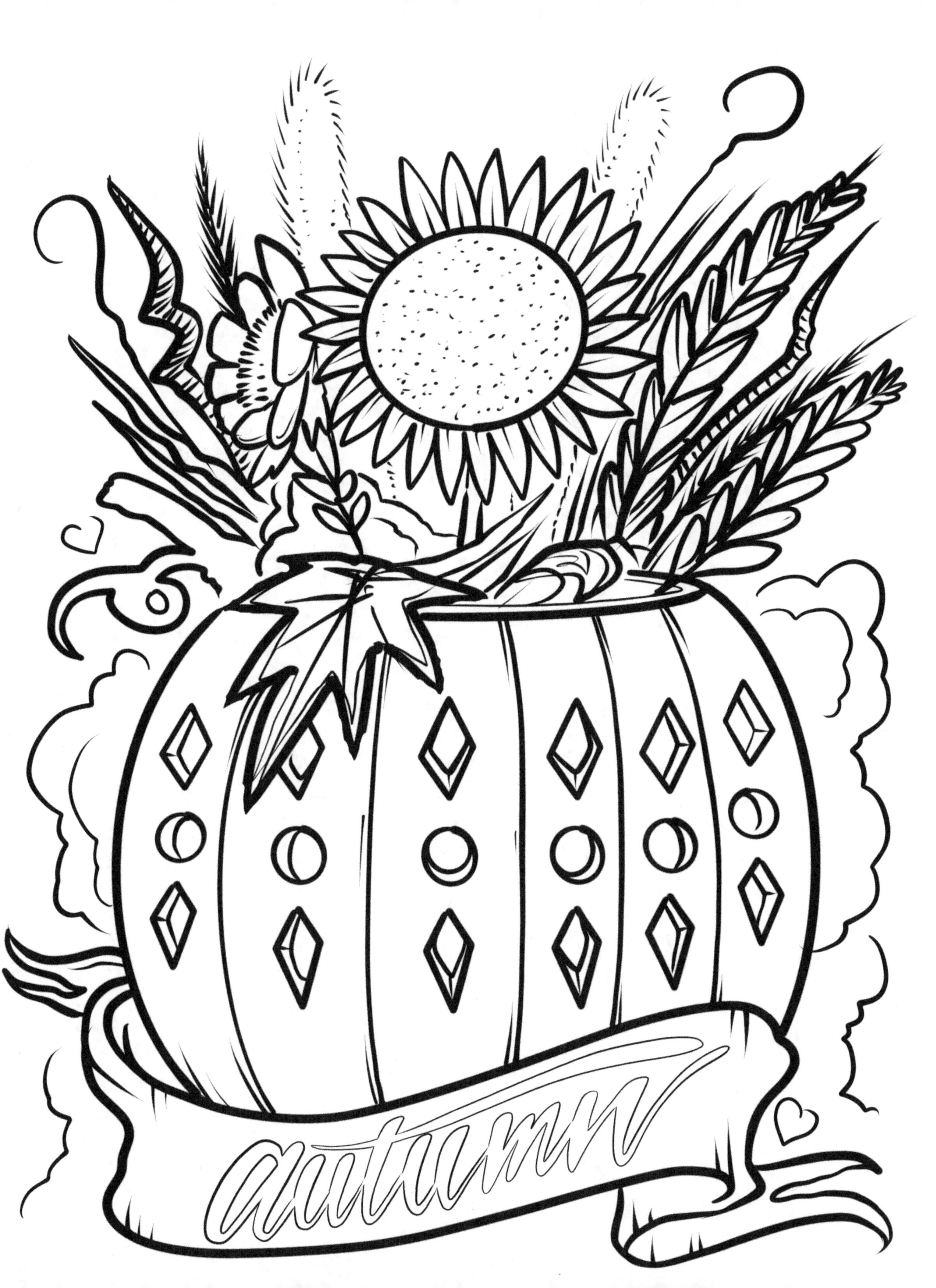
autumn

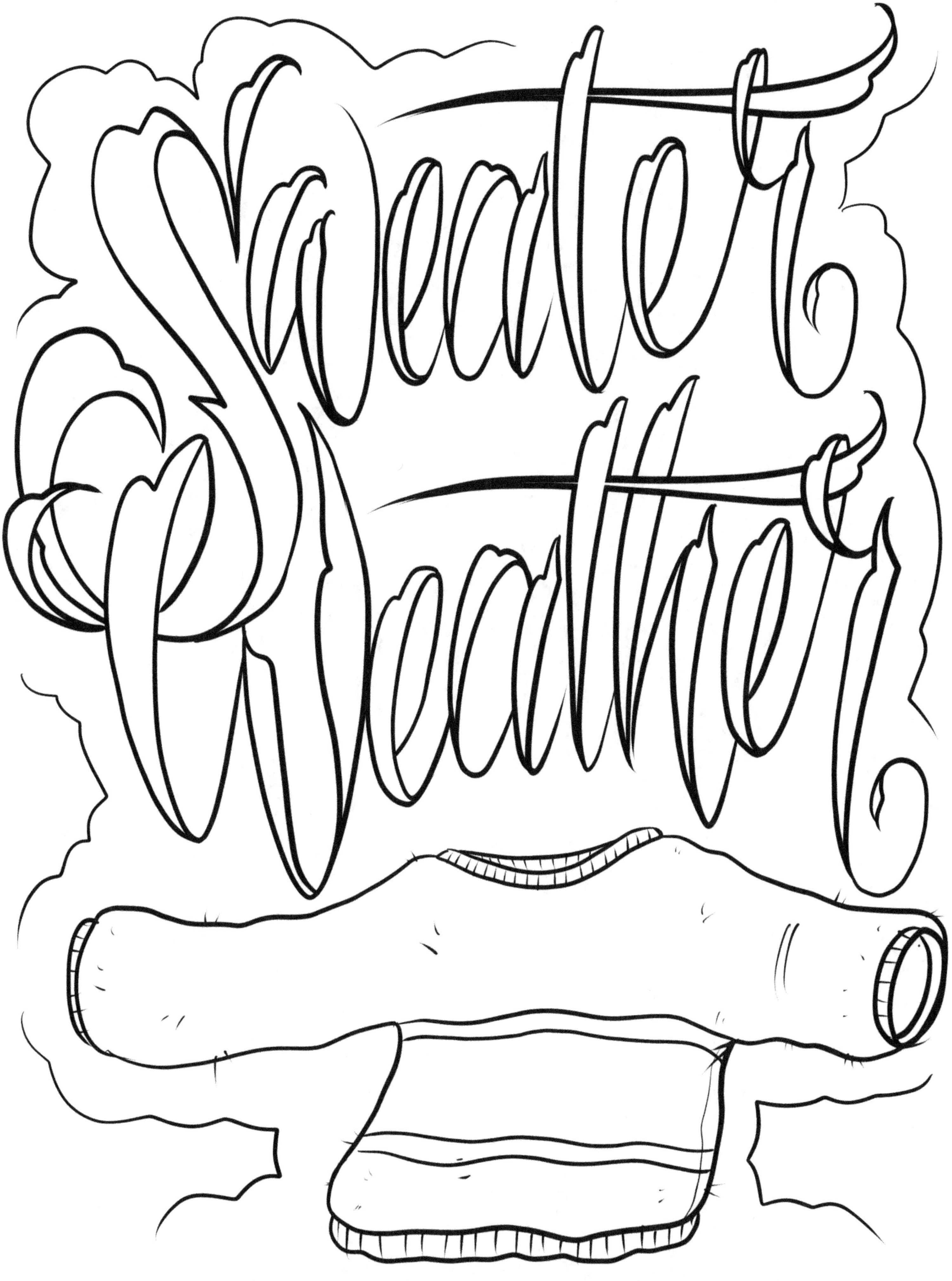
Sweater
Weather

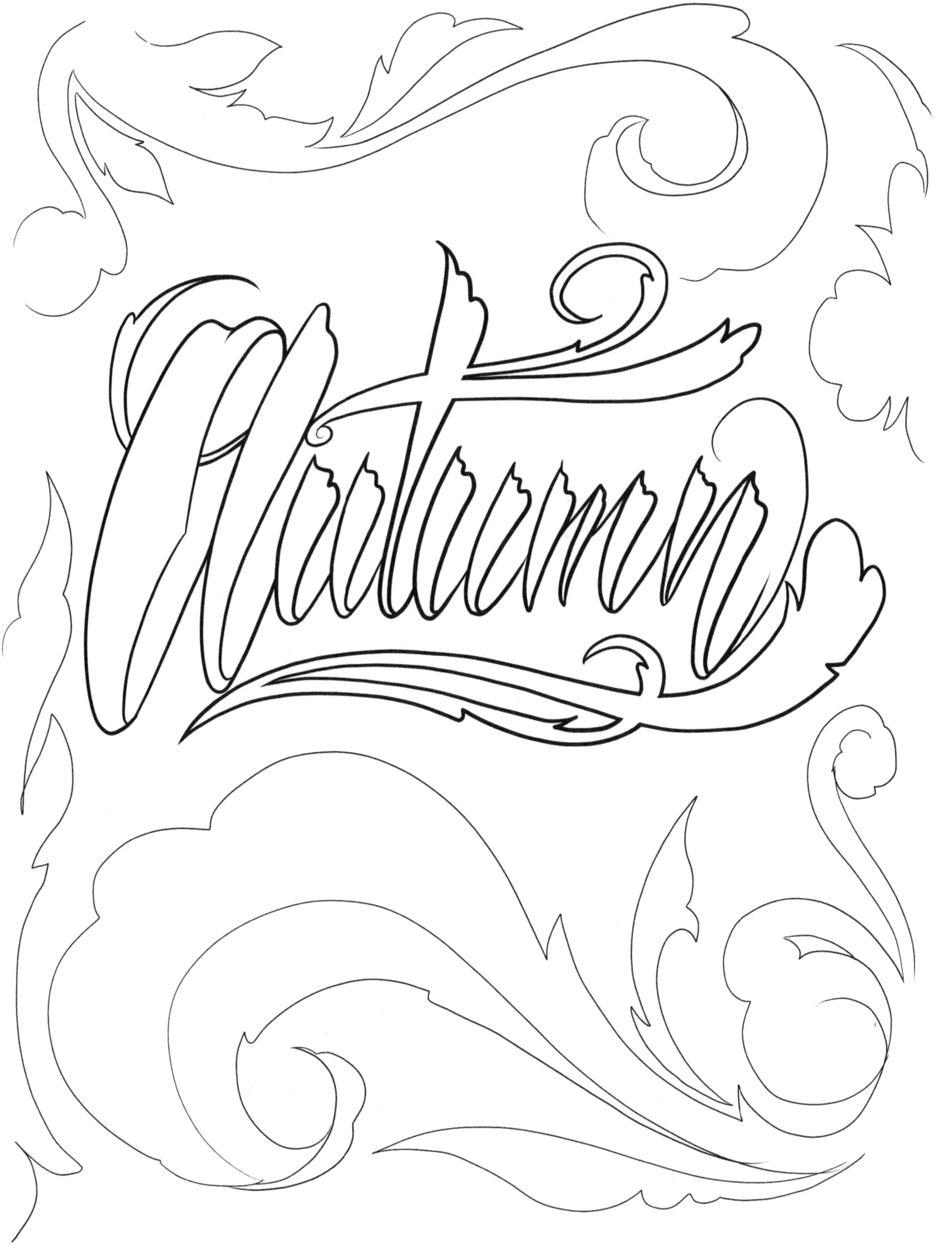
Autumn

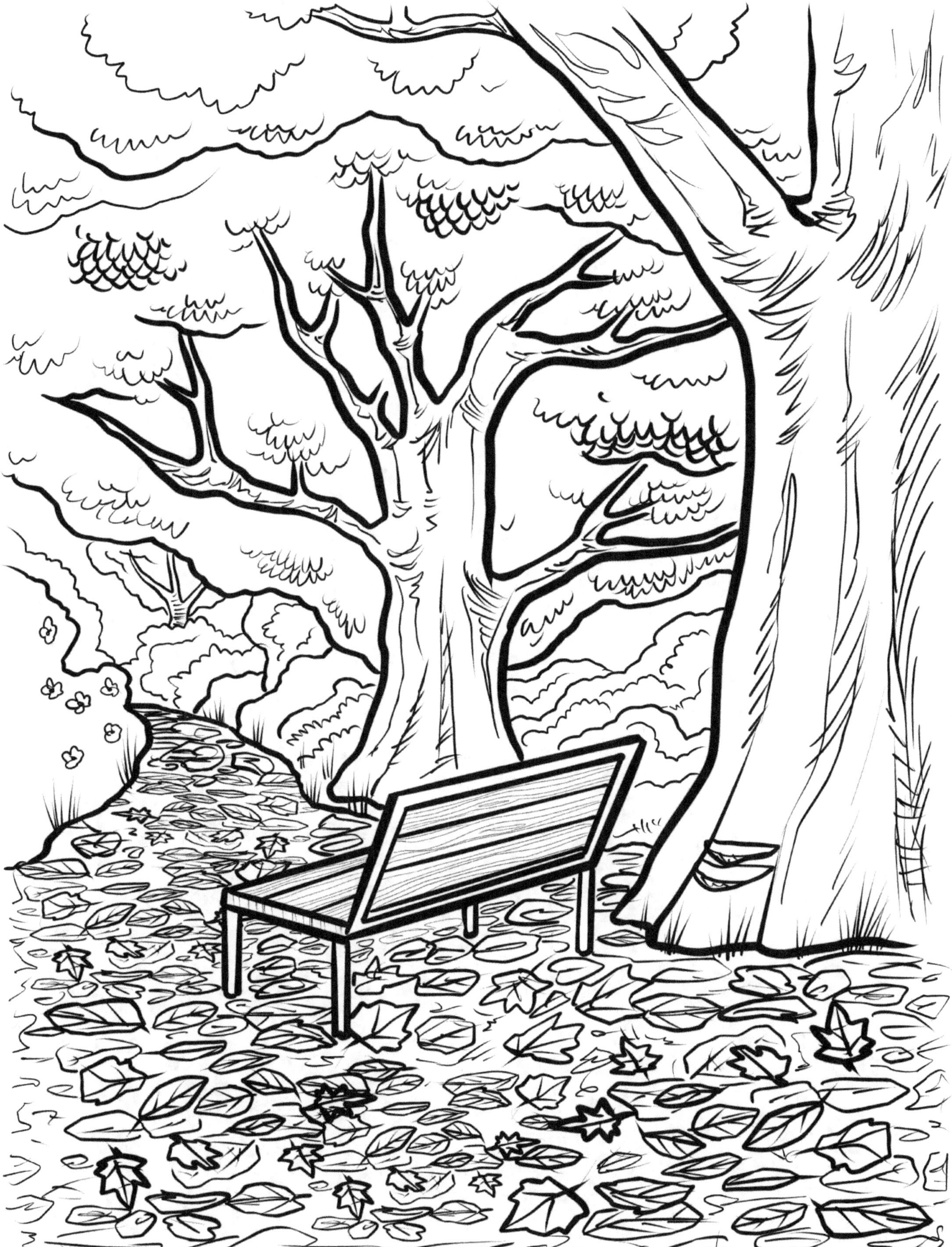

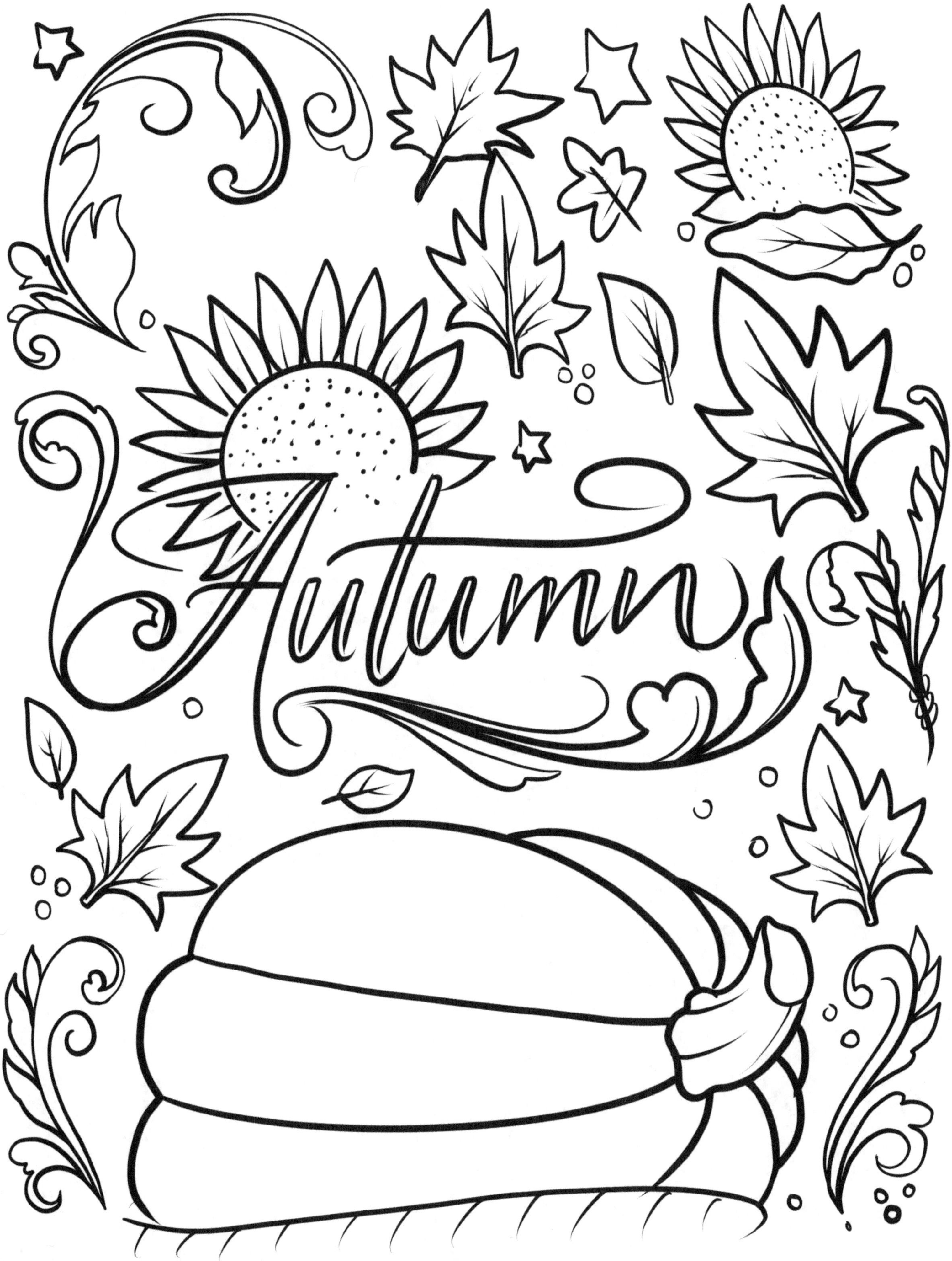
Autumn

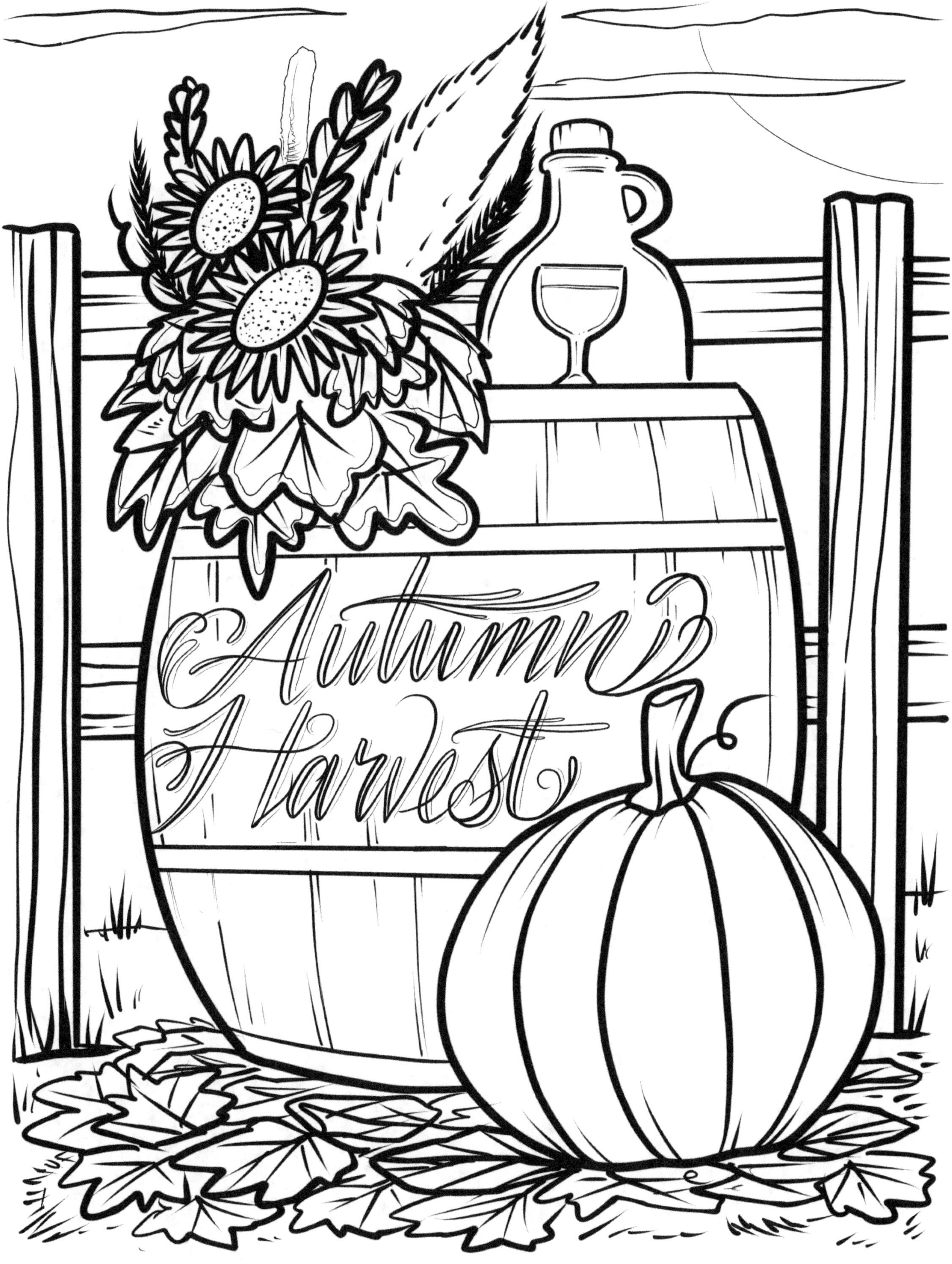
Autumn
Harvest

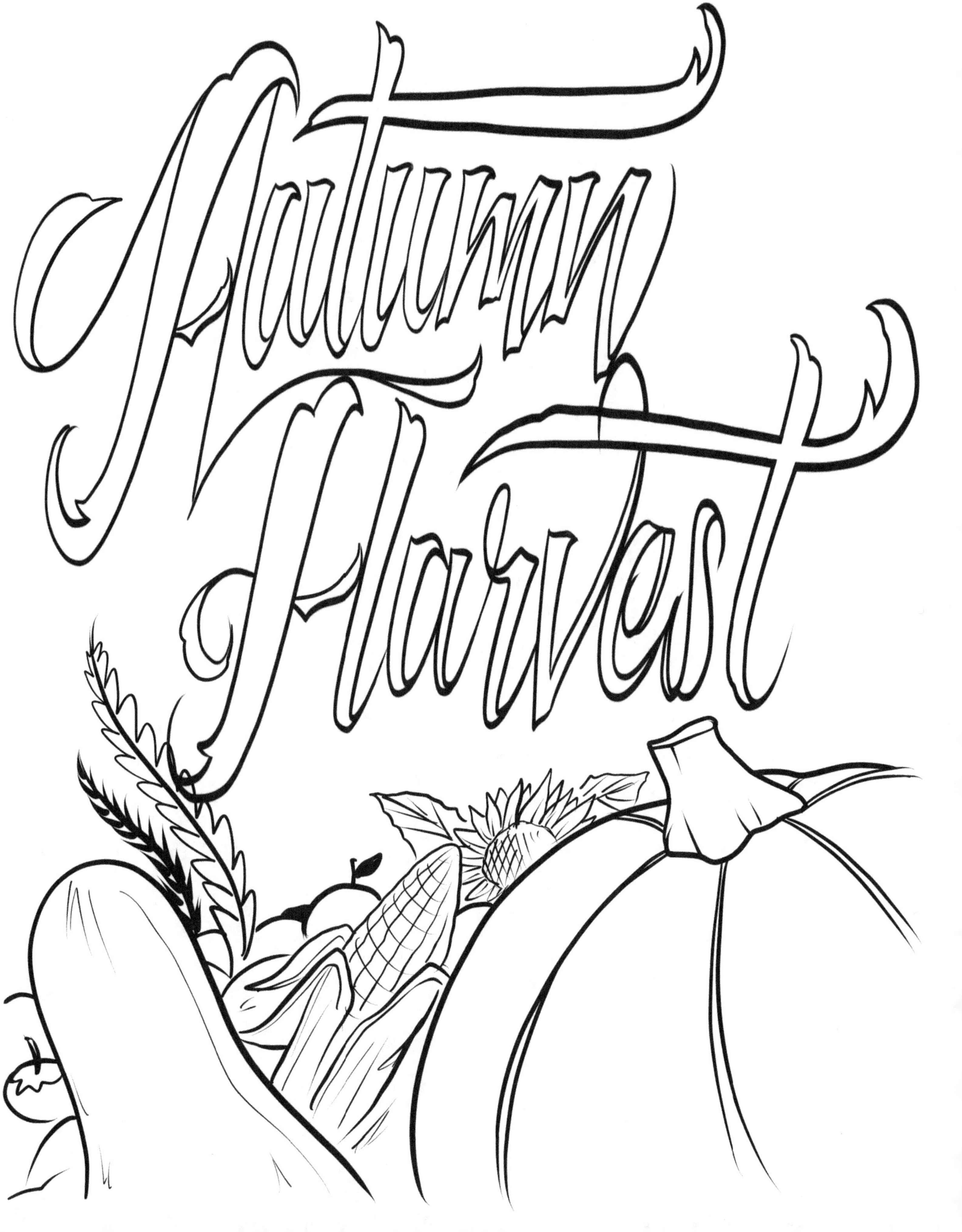
Autumn
Harvest

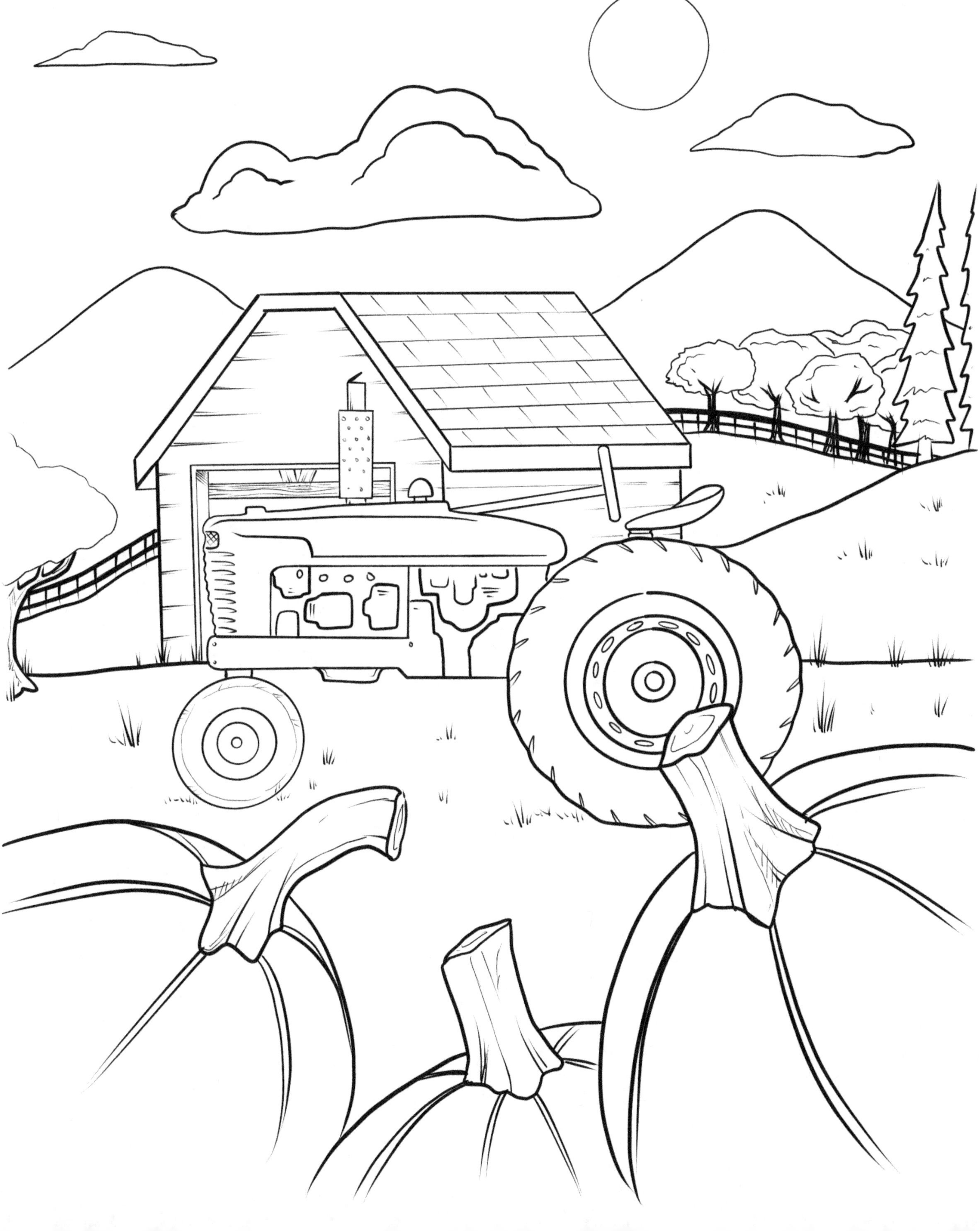

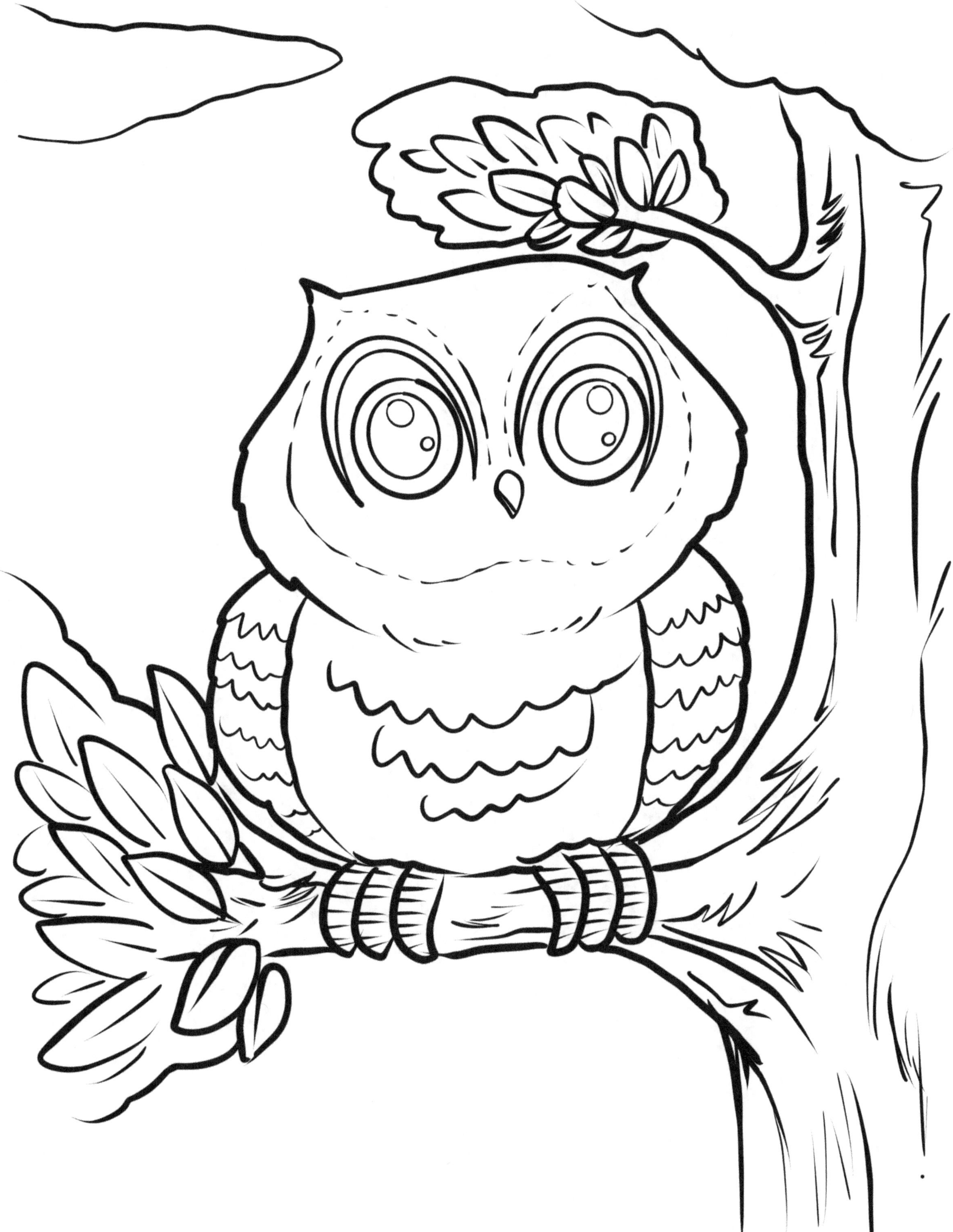

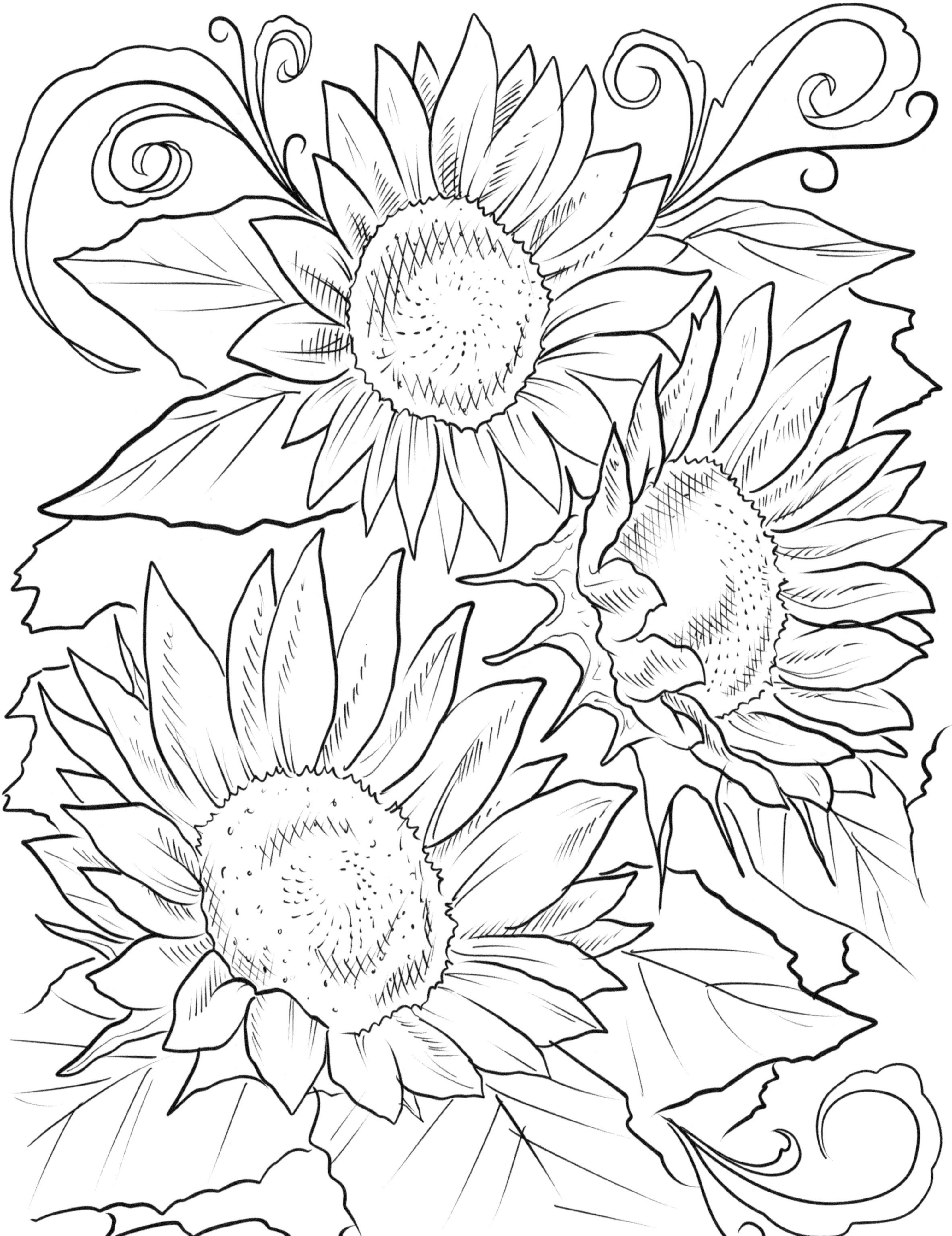

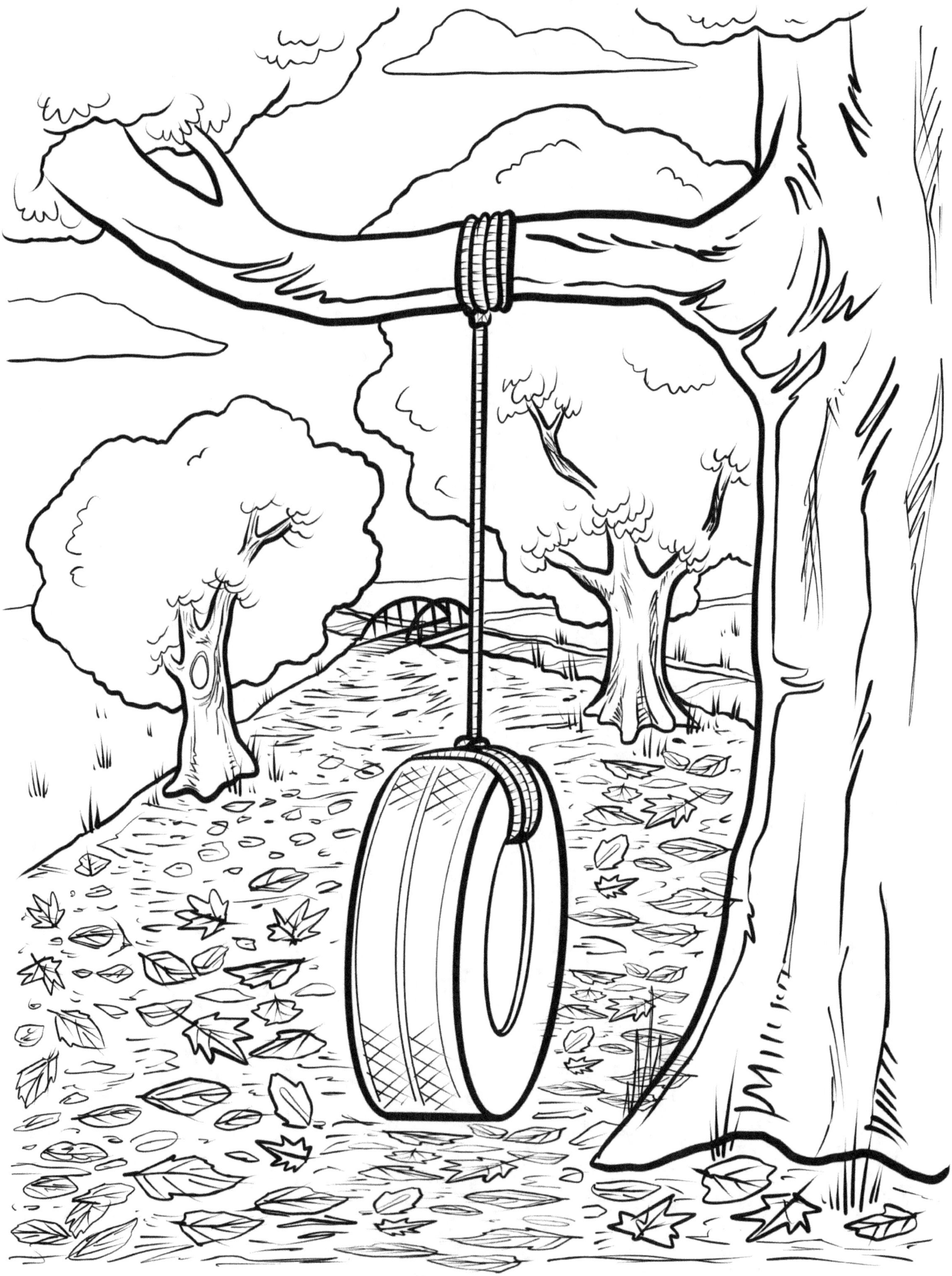

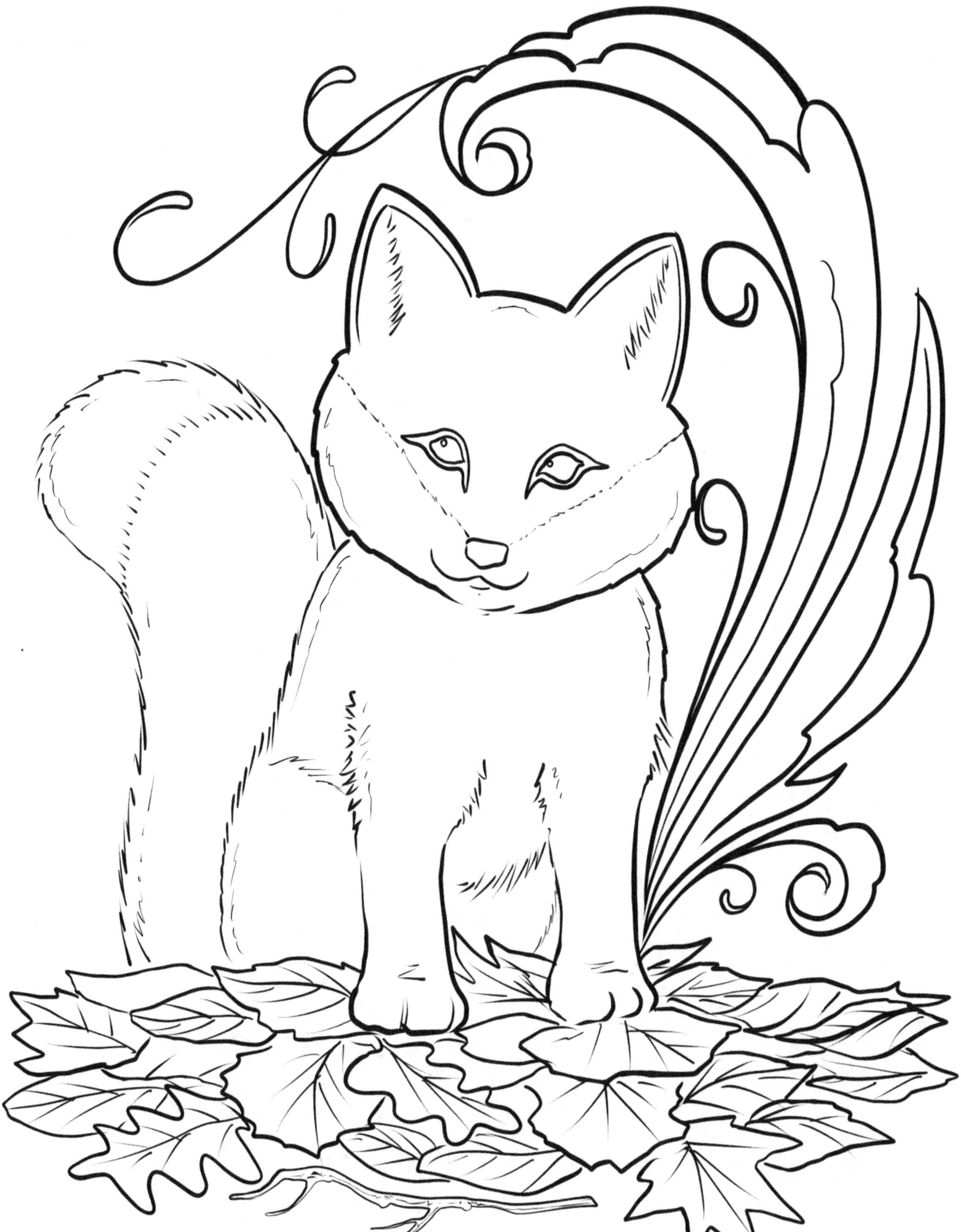

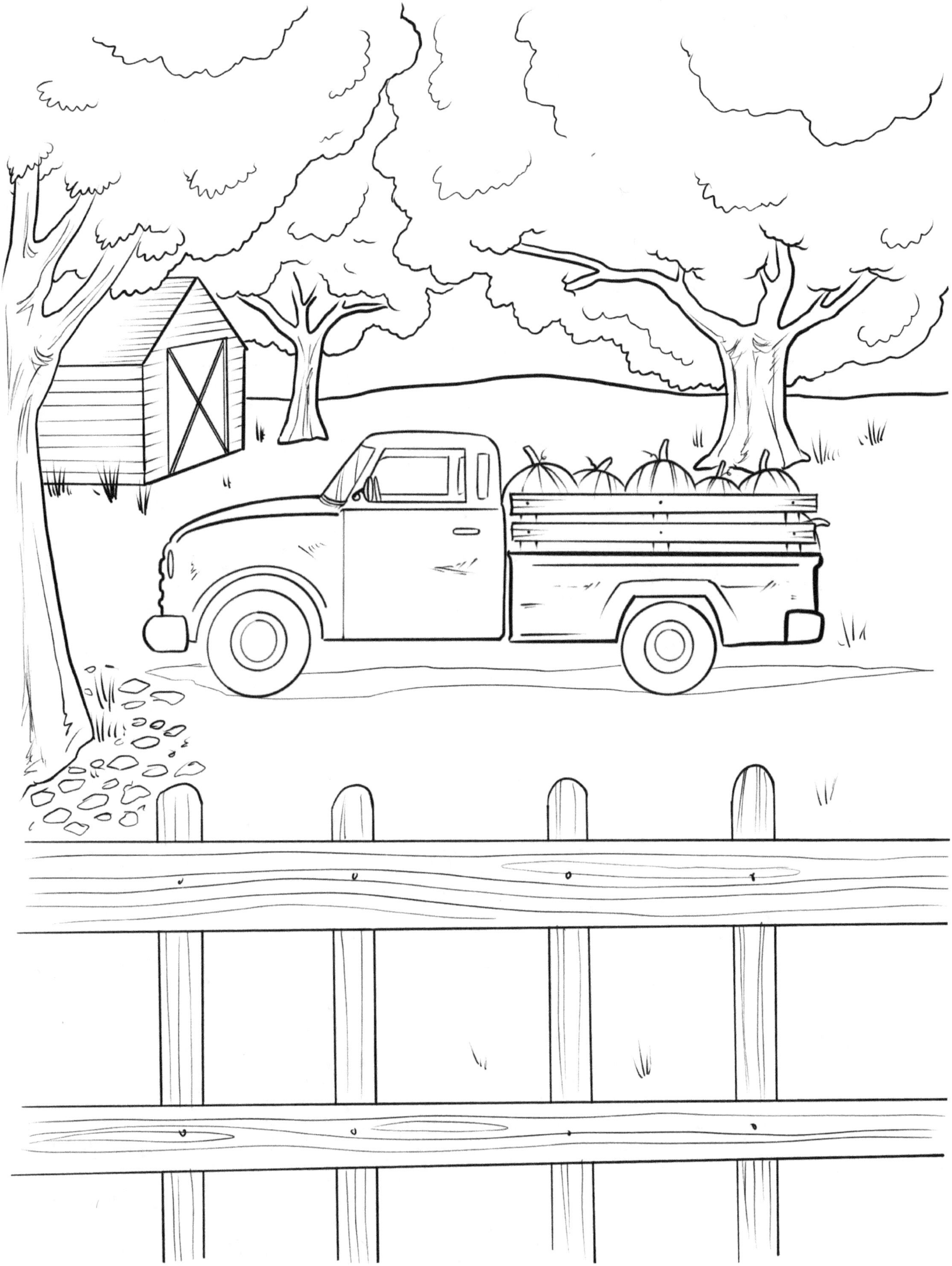

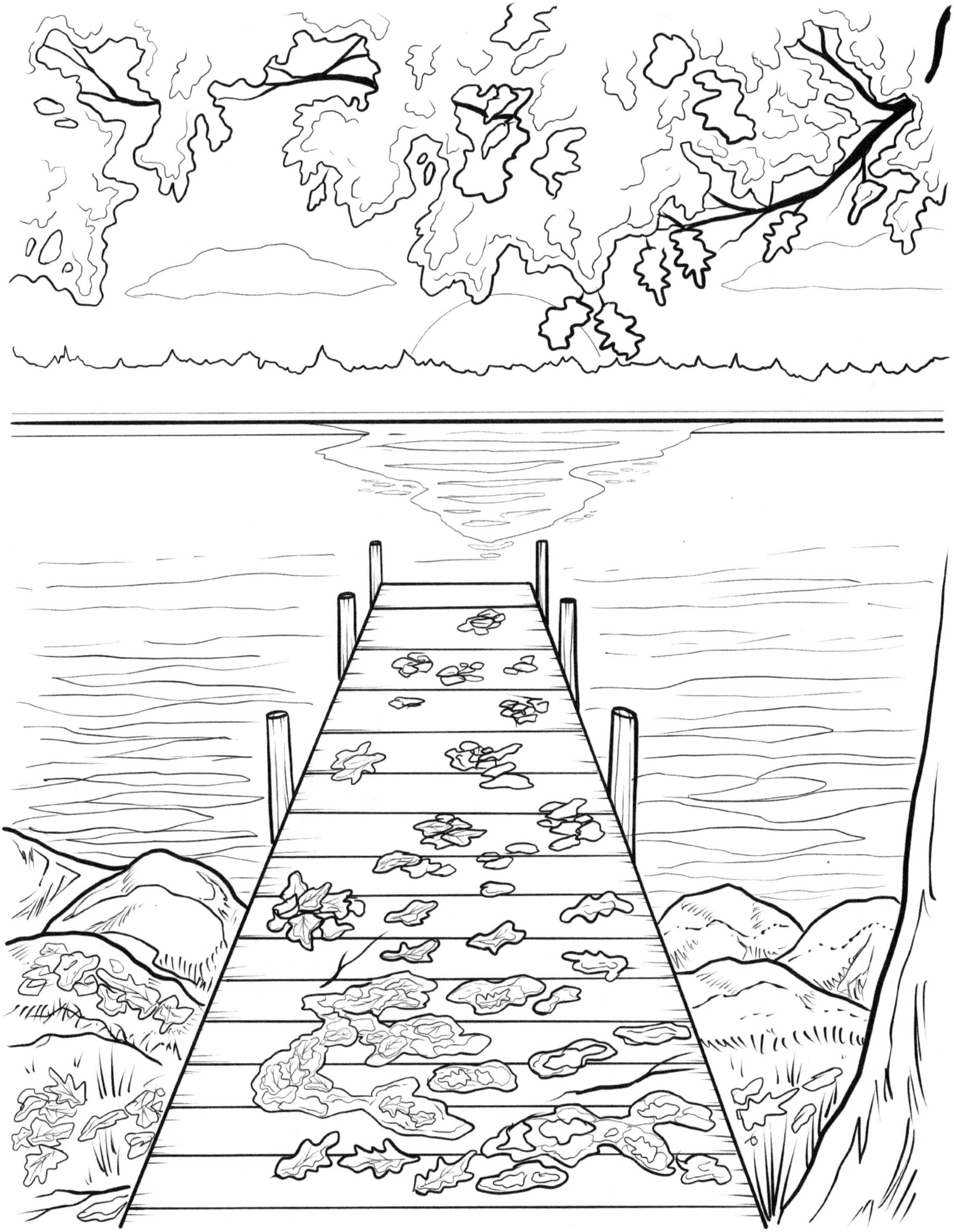

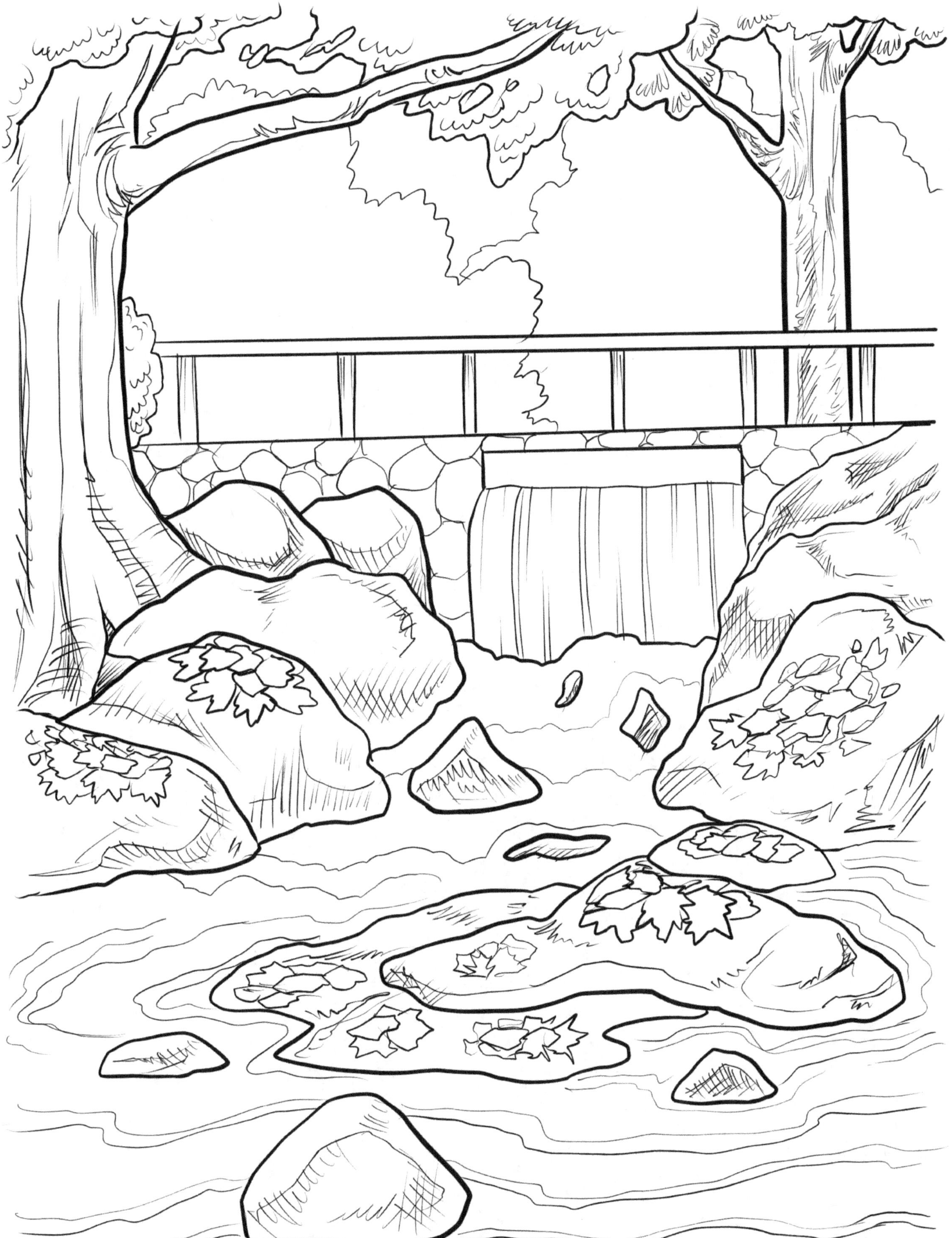

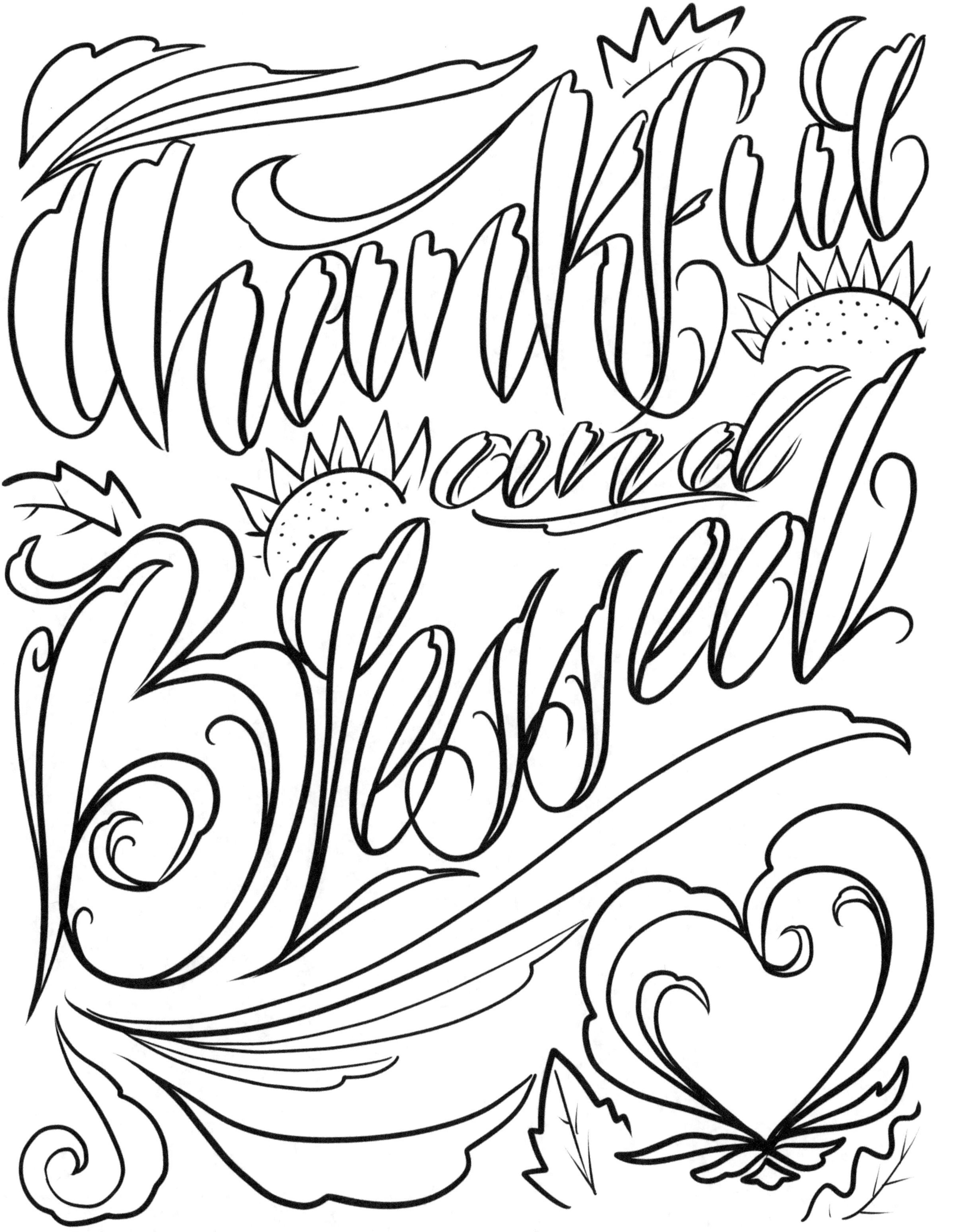
Thankful
and
Blessed

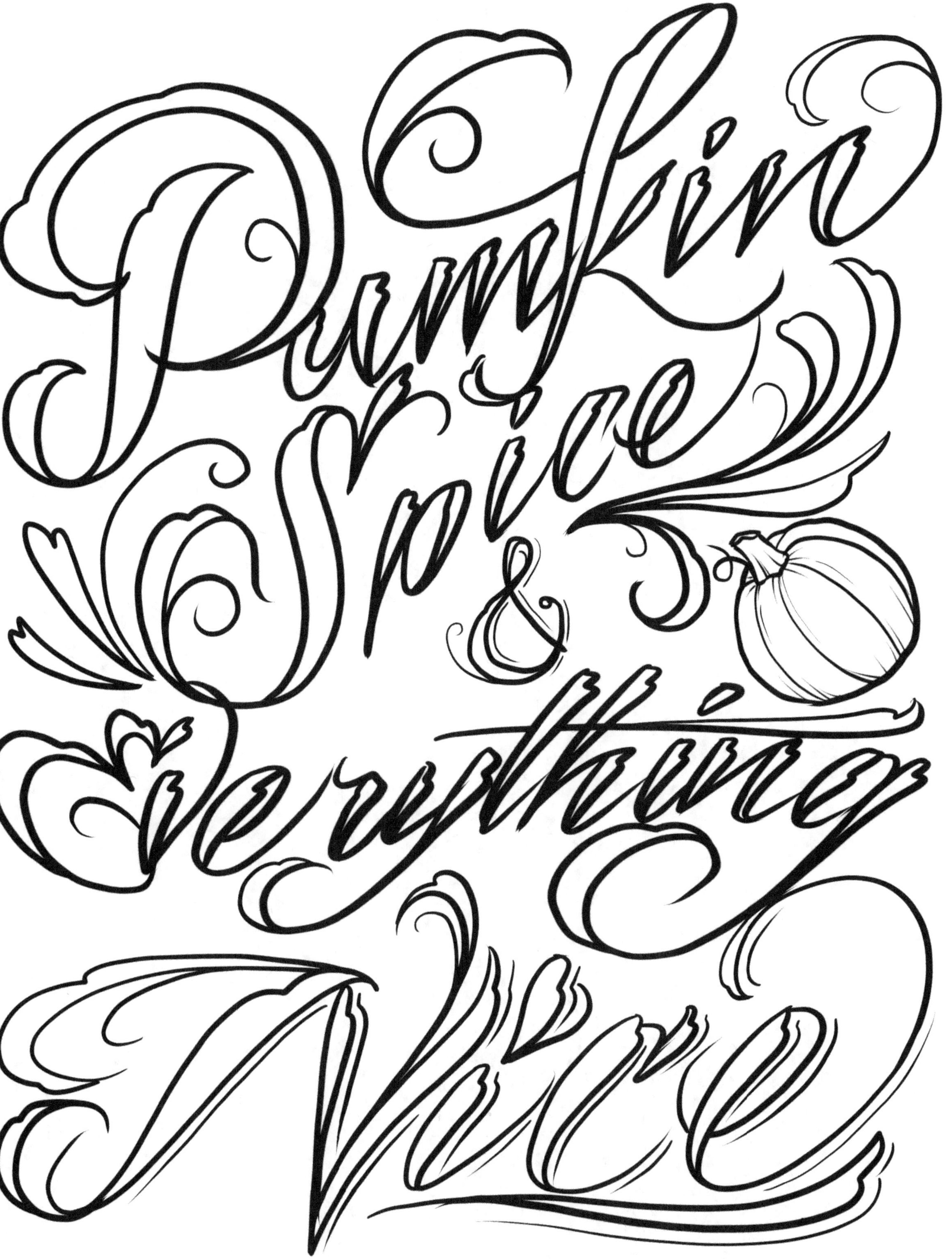
Pumpkin
Spice
&
Everything
Nice

www.ingramcontent.com/pod-product-compliance
Lightning Source LLC
Chambersburg PA
CBHW060006230526
45472CB00008B/1972
* 9 7 9 8 4 9 8 3 6 9 6 7 9 *